Katharine Yagi

What's Under that Log?

Bumblebee
Books

BUMBLEBEE PAPERBACK EDITION

A CIP catalogue record for this title is
available from the British Library.

ISBN: 978-1-83934-629-3

First Published in 2023

Olympia Publishers
Tallis House
2 Tallis Street
London
EC4Y 0AB

Printed in Great Britain

Dedication

I dedicate this book to my son, Félix. Always be curious.

When you're out on a walk, or a hike, or a jog,
you may see some neat critters in trees or under logs.
What might you find?   maybe a bird's chirp...
And apart from invertebrates it could be a herp!

Herps are amphibians and reptiles – a group that's diverse.
They are quite different though, let's look and converse!

Most amphibians are slimy and can breathe through their skin.
They lay eggs in the water and their babies must swim.

Most go through a change of body and style,
it is called "metamorphosis" and can take quite a while.

Some kinds of amphibians you see all the time,
like frogs, toads, and salamanders,
seen and heard in their prime.

Male frogs and toads sing in big groups to attract mates.
Springtime can be noisy when out very late!
Salamanders are silent but have a good plan.
They return to a pond to find mates if they can.

Now for the reptiles, these critters astound!
They have scales on their skin and lay eggs in
the ground.

They can be big or small and have lungs to breathe air.
Their homes are diverse and live almost anywhere!

They swim or crawl, and often they hide
Under brush, in trees or ponds... even on
the roadside.

You've likely seen reptiles everywhere when it's warm.
Like snakes, lizards, and turtles... That is the norm.

They're colourful and wonderful, especially when basking.
Then they're quick to run off to find food, then relaxing.

Do these groups have anything in common?
Why, yes! There's a term...

The environment controls their temperature.
They are called "ectotherms".

They use their behaviour to adjust as you see.
They are not always warm like you and me.

It's how they can live for so many years.
Slowing down when it's cold helps a lot, it appears.

Are any herps dangerous?
In Ontario, only some.
Rattlesnakes are venomous but we
have only one.

Massasaugas are rare, and shy,
and polite.
They rattle their tail when
having a fright!

It's a warning you see, to let us all know
that they might bite if you don't leave them alone.

The best thing to do here is to give them their space.
They'll crawl away soon. They won't go for the chase.

Their venom is used to catch prey in the field.
Any small mammal is very ideal.

Many other snakes look like them, you know...
And they copy their sounds, so predators don't show.

Snapping turtles are big with sharp claws and strong bite.

They're defending themselves when exposed or not right.

On the road we find snappers moving quite slow.
They've got somewhere in mind; they have places to go.

They're searching for space, more food, or new mates...
Or are females seeking a place to lay eggs.

If you see any turtle stopped
on the road,
Please help it across, safely
carry the load!

Are herps doing okay?

It depends where you look.
Where new houses are built, it is not
looking good.

Herps depend on their environments health to survive.

When wetlands are drained, they won't easily thrive.

How can I help? There's much we can do!
By living sustainably, this can help too.

Learning about wildlife and their needs are good stages.
Spread the word when you can! Be aware of the changes.

A message from the author about herp-searching etiquette:

While I love to encourage people to learn about herps, it is important to respect all animal habitats. Please be sure to return any logs or rocks that were lifted back to their original position so the critters can go back to their cozy homes.

Thanks for reading!

About the Author

I come from a family of six in Ontario, Canada, and am the eldest of four sisters. Having grown up with a biologist for a mother, I was naturally inclined to love nature and pursued a career in biology as well. After my son was born, I could see he has the same passion for nature and was inspired by his curiosity to write a children's book. I hope my writing inspires children around the world to learn more about our natural heritage and how to protect that legacy for future generations.

Acknowledgements

Thank you to my family for their encouragement and support in the production of this book. Heather, your artwork is beautiful, and I could not have done this without you!

Ingram Content Group UK Ltd.
Milton Keynes UK
UKHW050711040723
424461UK00003B/4